Dragons: Their History & Symbolism

Dragons
Their History
& Symbolism

Janet Hoult

GOTHIC IMAGE
PUBLICATIONS

First published 1978 as *A Short History of the Dragon*
This revised edition first published 1987
Second edition 1990
©Janet Hoult 1987

ISBN 0906362 09 1

Typesetting, drawings & cover by Janet Hoult

Printed by Sydney Lee (Exeter) Ltd.,
          Water Lane,
          Exeter, Devon
          EX2 8DC.

Published by Gothic Image Publications,
          7, High Street,
          Glastonbury,
          Somerset BA6 9DP.

Contents

Preface

The dragon is a symbol which is found all over the world, and dates from the earliest creation myths. It has many different meanings, and is portrayed in many different styles.

This book looks briefly at the depictions, history, celebrations, legends, heroes and saints connected with dragons, and the symbol's use in alchemy, as well as putting forward a suggestion or two as to what the dragon actually meant to people in the past.

Chapter 1

Definition of the Dragon

The dragon is a well known symbol all over the world, and although there are slight variations in its usual depiction (i.e. basically that of a large lizard with ears and wings), several main features are constant throughout. As the symbol is so widespread, I wondered when I first started to research the subject whether dragons could have actually existed on the earth at some time in the past, but had now become extinct. However, several years further on, I have found that there is no evidence for a theory of this kind at all. Dragons are not even a race memory dating back to the days of the cavemen and their encounters with dinosaurs, as over 60 million years separate the end of the dinosaur age with the beginning of mankind.

In previous centuries the case for dragons, as with many other mythical beasts, was more plausible, for nature was accepted unquestioningly as the work of God, existing solely for the use or teaching of man, and stories of fabulous foreign beasts, although only dubious hearsay, were taken as truth.

Early discoveries of fossilised dinosaur bones, and travellers' tales of Komodo dragons would have added further proof. Medieval bestiary writers such as Topsell, Gesner and Aldrovandi knew people who knew other people who had seen a dragon, and there was a thriving trade in fake baby dragons. These 'Jenny Hanivers' as they were called were lizards with bats' wings attached to them, and were imported from several countries, those from Japan being considered the best.

Yet dragons are found in mythology all over the world, and seem to symbolise a much wider range of meaning than could be covered by an extinct physical animal, or by a few bones discovered in one part of the world. Dragon legends and carvings spread from America, through Europe, India and China to New Zealand. The Chinese dragon is perhaps the most well known, symbolising fertility and wisdom, as well as being one of the signs of the Chinese horoscope. Celestial dragons live in the sky and carry the palaces of the gods on their backs; great sea dragons, three or four miles long live in the oceans, and when they rise to the surface cause typhoons. Subterranean dragons guard treasure hords deep in the earth, while terrestrial ones determine the course of streams and rivers, and are synomymous with *lung mei*, 'dragon lines' or lines of energy which run all over the countryside. In China's past, only members of the Imperial family were allowed to be buried on these invisible lines. Chinese emperors claimed that they were descended from dragons, and used a special five-clawed dragon emblem on their state robes.

The dragon is also found in North America. This dragon is taken from Wm. Dennis' drawing of 1825, of a figure about four feet high painted by Algonquin Indians on Piasa Rock, Illinois. In the Illini language, 'piasa' means the bird that devours men. The rock was later blown up by quarry men. It may not look much like the more usual pictures of dragons, but if we read the first written description of a dragon by Wang Fu, Chinese philosopher of the Han Dynasty, there are many similarities: It should have the horns of a stag, the head of a camel, long wiskers, the eyes of a demon, the neck of a snake, the scales of a carp, the claws of an eagle and the ears of a bull. The only great difference from many depictions of the British dragon is that the face of the American one is based on a human head rather than a lizard's.

So what are the characteristics of the British dragon? The basis of the symbol seems to have been a serpent, although the dragon has a much wider symbolism and more power than a mere snake. The origins of the serpent image may lie in the sacred snakes kept by the priestesses of the Earth-Mother religion, for in the creation myths of early civilisations in the Middle East the dragon symbolised the primal Mother.

In depictions, the dragon is distinguished from the serpent by several

A 'Jenny Haniver' from Edward Topsell's 'Historie of Foure-Footed Beastes', London 1607.

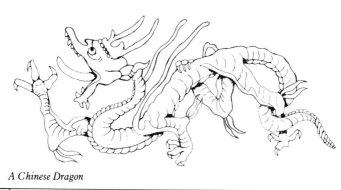

A Chinese Dragon

Wm. Dennis's drawing of a dragon depicted on a rock at Piasa, Illinois.

physical differences, such as the addition of ears, horns or a plume, or perhaps having legs or wings.

Most dragons have a loop in their tails, as if to symbolise the energy they are associated with.

In Britain there are two main types of dragon: the land and air variety, and sea-dragons, the 'nicor'. 'Dragon' and 'nicor' have different origins, but can be used to describe the same beast, as in the legend of Beowulf, in which Grendel's mother, the dragon at the bottom of the lake, is described by both names.

The Anglo-Saxon word 'drakan' is probably a Greek derivative, either from 'draco' meaning a dragon or large snake, or from the verb 'derkein', which means to see clearly. Dragons were credited with clear sight, wisdom and the ability to foretell the future.

'Nicor' seems to be the Anglo-Saxon term for any strange beast that came out of water. According to the *Anglo-Saxon Dictionary* (Bosworth & Taylor), 'nicor' can also mean a hippopotamus or a crocodile, while the Icelandic word 'nyker' means a sea-goblin.

A sea serpent from Edward Topsell's 'Historie of Foure-Footed Beastes', London 1607.

It is possible that sea-dragons do physically exist, as there many well-authenticated sightings of sea-serpent and lake monsters - the most famous of these being the Loch Ness Monster. Could they be remnants from the age of the dinosaur? Recently a high-speed camera under the water of Loch Ness with a sonar device to trigger the shutter has produced two photographs of what could be the fin of an underwater dinosaur, a plesiosaur. And in Lake Tele, in the Congo, 450 miles into the jungle come reports of a brontosaur-like animal, the 35ft long 'Mokele Mbembe'. Seen by Herman Rogustus, amongst others in 1981, he reports that it had a long tail which extended to about 15 ft.

British land dragons are called by various names, including Orme, Worm or Vurm, originating from the Norse word 'ormr' meaning dragon, and seem to be used to describe wingless dragons.

Remains of dragon traditions can be found in many areas of Britain in the names of places, even though any legend may be lost. Examples are at Drakelow in Derbyshire - whose name in AD 942 was 'Draca Hlowe', meaning dragon mound - and Wormingford (Essex), Wormsley (Hereford), Ormskirk (Lancashire) and Ormiston (Lothian).

Greek jar, c. 470-460 B.C.   *Greek dish, c. 480-490 B.C.*

In Greece the early differences between a 'draco' meaning either a snake or a dragon are confused, as the same word meant either. But the legends changed with time, or varied in content from area to area, and so did the shape and symbolism of the 'draco', as can be seen and compared in the two known illustrations of the legend of the Golden Fleece. The first depiction, painted around 470-460 BC shows the 'draco' as a snake, while in the second, painted a decade or two earlier, a dragon is depicted, and the whole symbolism shows a deeper meaning which has disappeared from the legend as it has come down to us. It indicates a connection with rejuvenation or rebirth as practised in the religion of the Goddess, especially in connection with initiation ceremonies - another important part of dragon symbolism. This major link between dragons and the Mother appears time and again, and still continues in modern usage, where dominant women are labelled as dragons.

It is obvious that dragon symbolism has many branches, but the strongest is that it seems to represent the natural energy of the elements and of the earth and sky. The energy of the earth is that of the fertility of the land and the natural currents in the earth, which can probably be directed by earthworks;

while that of the sky is seen in the different and strange forms which electrical 'static' energy can take such as ball lightning or UFOs.

The dragon came to symbolise the religion which worshipped and used those energies. Sometimes seemingly evil or negative things such as human sacrifice may have been practised, and, unfortunately the whole religion was identified with these and labelled as evil by rival conquering religions, and then Christianity. The priests of one religion will seize on anything they can to condemn another, a fact all too apparent today.

Another branch of symbolism connected with dragons lies in the realm of archetypes, first explored by psychologist C. G. Jung. Seen from this angle, the dragon may be a manifestation on another plane of existance. In this type of area the dividing line between the 'real' and the 'imaginary' is very unclear, for the description of an archetype sounds very like the qualities of a thinking being from another level, such as a god or a deva, or an elemental form. The archetype, so Erich Neumann, colleague of Jung writes in his book *The Great Mother*, is a nuclear phenomenon transcending consciousness'. It usually cannot be seen, but acts as a 'magnetic' field which affects the mind through instincts, and brings subconscious material to the surface of the mind by the use of symbols.

If thought-forms or archetypes are able to manifest to some people as physical or semi-physical forms, then in some cases dragons can be said to exist.

Chapter 2

Dragon History & Ceremonies

In the course of time, the dragon came to symbolise the religion which worshipped the natural energies of the earth and sky, the first of all religions - that of the Great Goddess. The first dragons in both legend and depiction were the Mothers of the Earth. Tiamat of Babylonia is the earliest example. In the Babylonian creation myth she was the primal being, and after she had been killed by the warrior-god Marduk - because the gods wanted power for themselves - heaven and earth were created from her body.

Geographically, the nearest piece of evidence to Britain that we have of the early Mother Goddess' association with the dragon was found at Fardol, in Northern Jutland, Denmark. This is a Bronze-Age figurine of a goddess and a dragon. The goddess has a hole in her hand, the dragon a hole in his mouth, and the position in which they were found indicates that they were looped together.

The killing, or in some cases staking of the primal dragon occurs in the

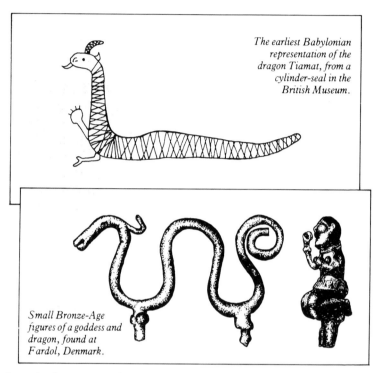

The earliest Babylonian representation of the dragon Tiamat, from a cylinder-seal in the British Museum.

Small Bronze-Age figures of a goddess and dragon, found at Fardol, Denmark.

legends of many countries.

One of the main interpretations which has been put forward is that the story is symbolic of Goddess-worshipping tribes being overrun by the more warlike Indo-European male-god-worshipping tribes. This can be seen clearly in many legends.

In India, for example, Indra killed the Mother Goddess Danu and her son Vritra - described as serpent demons - in order to become supreme in heaven. We know that this is a symbolic account of the conquest of a people and their religion, because we have historical evidence that the Goddess-worshipping Dravidian race became the lowest caste in India, the 'untouchables'. They were regarded as less than human, and their lesser gods, serpent-dragons symbolising wisdom, called Nagas, became demons. The race tended to take the name 'Naga' for themselves too.

In Armenia, 'vishaps' is the name given to the earlier race, their dragon-like gods, and the stones which they erected to mark the source of irrigation

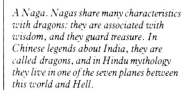

A Naga. Nagas share many characteristics with dragons: they are associated with wisdom, and they guard treasure. In Chinese legends about India, they are called dragons, and in Hindu mythology they live in one of the seven planes between this world and Hell.

systems. The members of this early race could apparently appear as both humans and serpents and could soar into the air with the help of oxen. They date back to the pre-Armenian ascendancy, before the coming of the Medes, Persians and Greeks.

Two traditions about Delphi, most famous of Greek oracles suggest there was a conflict there. One legend tells of a dragon which ravaged the countryside around Delphi, which was killed by the sun-god Apollo. An earlier tradition is that the Pythia, the oracle, used to sit with a serpent, the intermediary between this world and the underworld, coiled round her stool. Was this the 'draco' that had to be killed?

There is an echo of this story in the Beowulf legend. Beowulf killed the monster Grendel, and then went to kill his dragon mother, who lived at the bottom of a lake.

But the strangest and most contrived version of the story is that of Adam and Eve in the Old Testament. The serpent of Eden may well have been the Goddess. Isis, Great Goddess of Egypt, was symbolised by a snake and sometimes was depicted as a human headed snake by the Romans. This tradition was continued by Medieval painters who portrayed the serpent of Eden as a female-headed snake. Adam's first wife, Lilith (whom we read about in Jewish rabbinical texts) had probably succumbed to this other religion and had rivalled him for power. For this she was labelled as a demon. Eve threatened to turn the same way when she wanted the knowledge of good and evil, but by teaching Jewish women about the 'original sin', the fathers of the Jewish faith ensured that no woman was officially allowed to think or question for herself, and thus would not be led astray by any rival religion, especially one that had a female deity. Some Gnostic sects in the early days of the Christian Church, however, praised Eve for bringing wisdom to mankind.

Detail from a miniature of the Garden of Eden, from 'Les Tres Riches Heures du Duc de Berri' before 1416.

Drawing from a Gnostic manuscript showing the Garden of Eden.
*   The half serpent/half woman symbol appears quite often in medieval painting and Gnostic works, and is called a Melusina, a half human/half fairy/dragon.*

The derogation of former deities into devils by a conquering religion can also be seen in the way that Christianity turned the Graeco-Roman nature god Pan into their other main symbol for the Devil, that of the horned and cloven-hooved Satan.

However, there is another angle to this story of dragon-killing which can be glimpsed from depictions of dragons and hints in legends and ceremonies which were continued until recently in this country, which is that instead of killing the dragon, the heroes are staking it. By doing this, they are guiding the energies of the dragon, which in this sense is synonymous with the energies of the earth. This channelling of the flow of energies is implied by an Egyptian drawing of the staking of the great serpent Apep. The knives do not so much pierce him as guide him.

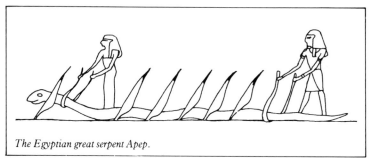

The Egyptian great serpent Apep.

The basic analogy is that the staking of the dragon - the beast or symbolic form of the Earth Goddess - is like staking the earth. In his book *The Lost Language of Symbolism*, Harold Bayley says that George, the name of the most famous dragon-killer, could mean 'ge-urge', with 'ge' meaning the earth, and 'urge' meaning to urge or stimulate the earth. The Greek name George means a 'husbandman' or a 'tiller of the earth'. St. George's Day, April 23rd, is just the right time to stimulate the earth at the end of winter, ready to plant the crops and encourage their growth, signified by the fertility celebrations of 1st May. There are several things done in spring which look like staking the earth: even such a task as stabbing the earth with a dibber in order to plant seedlings resembles it.

During the Middle Ages the time of year from St. Georges Day to Ascension Day used to see many parades and celebrations connected with the coming of Spring, both in Britain and all over the Continent. The main figures in these processions varied. Sometimes there was a dragon - with or without a St. George; or a giant, perhaps a relic of an old nature god and a variant of the 'Green Man'. Other characters may have included a giantess, the wife of the giant, and various animals such as the hobby hoss - the main character still retained at the Padstow procession. Smaller effigies - such as the dragons and the hobby hoss consist of a wicker frame covered with painted canvas, which could be carried by one man. The larger giants needed several men to support them inside, and they would be moved along by ropes, resting on rollers. These would then be paraded through the streets of the town amidst singing, dancing and general revelry. The last of these giants was found mouldering in a hall in Salisbury in 1844. In Britain many dragon effigies were given a veneer of Christianity by adopting the George and dragon theme. These were once very widespread but are now mostly forgotten. A couple, in Norwich and Leicester were continued up until the last century, and part of the Helston Furry Dance, held in May every year, includes a moving mummers play with a dragon.

Various legends are given to explain the Furry Dance. According to folklorist William Henderson, writing in 1879, the celebration commemorates an occasion when the town was threatened by a fiery dragon, carrying in his claws a red hot ball. The dragon finally flew on and dropped the ball half a mile away. When dancing the Furry Dance, he says, one party of dancers went off to the moor before dawn and began to dance from the spot when dawn arose. The ball is supposed to be in the yard of the principal hotel.

Nowadays, the first dance starts at 7 o'clock, but from dawn (around 6.30) till 7 o'clock the church bells are rung. There do not seem to be the remains of a ball in the hotel yard, but what there is, embedded in the wall of 'The Angel' is the 'Hell Stone', purported to have been thrown at St. Michael by the Devil with whom he was having a battle. The stone appears to be a large old millstone.

The Flora Day Association and Stewards of the Helston Furry Dance give three legends concerning St. Michael fighting the Devil as the basis for the celebrations. In one, St. Michael threw a large stone at the Devil, who then fell beaten into Loe Pool, while in another the Devil threw the stone lid of Hell at St. Michael to topple him from his Cornish Mount, but it missed and fell at Helston. A more down-to-earth version tells of a plague which swept through Helston, making the people leave their homes and live in the woods. When the plague died down, they returned waving flowers and dancing.

The dragon enters the celebrations in the Hal-an-Tow, which is performed at certain points in the town beginning at 8.30 in the morning, between sessions of the Furry Dance, which is a long processional dance.

The Hal-an-Tow is similar to the old May Eve celebrations when the young people of the town went into the woods to spend the night there. In this case the young people go out ostensibly to collect boughs of sycamore. There are many associations with pagan fertility rites in these celebrations, not least the steady, mystical beat of the Furry Dance. At the first dance in the morning, before the town is crowded with tourists, the sound of the steady beat as the procession climbs one of the main streets creates a very powerful atmosphere.

The celebrations in the towns such as Norwich, Leicester and Burford consisted of parading large wicker effigies of dragons and sometimes giants through the streets of the town amidst general revelry. They were very old ceremonies, with their origins back in pagan times, and were usually held on the three days preceding Ascension Day - the Festival of Rogation. During these three days church officials and clergy, together with the inhabitants of the town walked the parish boundaries, and at specific points stopped and prayed for blessings on the earth and for protection against evil. The places where the dragon was put during these prayers came to be known as the dragon's rock or the dragon's stone. At the end of the three days the dragon was beaten and kicked - perhaps a kind of 'scapegoat' to atone for the sins of the people.

At Norwich, the dragon Snap was paraded through the streets for three days, and two of the dragons used now hang in the Castle Museum at Norwich - resplendent in green and gold canvas. The older of the two, the Civic Snap

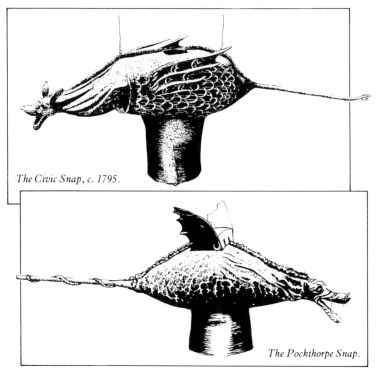

The Civic Snap, c. 1795.

The Pockthorpe Snap.

dates from around 1795, and opposite hangs the Pockthorpe Snap, made by the people of this neighbouring village for use in their own similar celebrations.

The procession originated in 1408 when the Norwich Guild of St. George agreed to "furnish priests with copes, and the George shall go in procession and make conflict with the dragon, and keep his estate both days". This guild was a charitable and religious one, its objectives being "to the honour of St. George and his feast, the worship of God, and prayers for the bretheren and sisters of the fraternity living and departed, and for all men travaillian in ye King's viage".

So the procession was supplied with clothing and armour for St. George "gilt with crest, and three ostrich feathers", a "sword covered with velvet", some banners and "a dragon".

However, although the dragon was supposed to be beaten after the festival, he quickly became the most popular figure. Through the years of the Middle Ages, the series of dragon effigies became very grand: their wings flapped, having horseshoes for gums enabled them to open and close their mouths with with a resounding clack (earning them the nickname of 'old Rustyguts'), and gunpowder was used to make them belch smoke and fire. One account reads "2/4 for the man playing the dragon with gunpowder. 10/- for making a new dragon".

Snap became so popular that in the years following the Reformation, although the St. George and the maiden were dropped from the procession, the dragon continued, and towards the end of his career, in the 19th century, even headed the Lord Mayor's Procession - although he was not always well-behaved, and would try to snatch the caps from boys' heads, for which they would have to pay a forfeit. The Civic Snap was last used in 1850 and now hangs in retirement in the Keep. After 1850, up until the First World War, the Pockthorpe dragon was used when a processional dragon was needed, and was brought out again during the Festival of Britain in 1951.

The procession in Leicester was called the 'Riding of the George', and was the 'grandest solemnity of the town', in which everyone took part, and people came from the neighbouring vilages to join in. Little is said of the dragon, except for one entry in the records for 1536, which says that the chamberlains of the town 'paid for the dressing of the dragon, 4s'.

Another variation of Spring celebrations used to be found at Kinnoul Hill in Perth, Scotland. The people there held 'superstitious games' on May 1st each year actually outside the 'Dragon's Hole' until the Reformers banned them, so Henry Adamson, writing in 1638, tells us.

The Chinese hold dragon processions to mark the new year, and to ask for

An eastern processional dragon.

fertility and rain, and these, like the British ones were, are accompanied by lots of noise and dancing, to give the Spring a good welcome.

Dragon processions were an important part of celebrations in the ancient world also, the best example being the Hittites. Every year they re-enacted the killing or staking of the dragon Illuyankas by the weather-god, at the Purulli festival. This was probably the most important festival of the year, for King Mursilis II was required to leave off a military campaign on one occasion in order to return to his capital and preside over the festival.

'Purulli' means of the earth, and although the details have been lost, the linking of names is useful, and further implies that the staking of the dragon symbolises the awakening of the earth ready for the rebirth of the Spring. The festival took place in the mausoleum of the temple of Lilwani, an earth goddess.

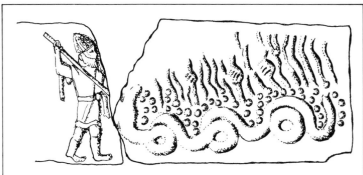

The staking of the dragon Illuyankas, a bas-relief from the Lion Gate, Malatya, North Syria.

Such Spring celebrations were very widespread geographically and historically, and *The Golden Bough* by Sir James Frazer is full of examples.

But there is a darker side to some of these earth/fertility celebrations, which to us seems not festive at all - the practice of human sacrifice.

The matriarch of the tribe or country, as the personification of the Earth-Mother, changed her consort every year, or several years. This 'year king' would be married in the Spring, and his year with the queen would follow the seasons, for in the Summer and Autumn he would hope to make her fruitful, lie dormant in Winter, then be sacrificed in Spring and his remains ploughed into the soil to make the ground fruitful. In many cases the enactment was symbolic, but in some, this or a similar sacrifice would have been actually carried out.

It would seem a savage custom to a conquering male-deity-based race, who killed mainly in battle and in quarrels, and it is probably the main reason why the dragon, as a symbol of the Earth Mother religion, was looked on as evil, female, and a destroyer of men.

Chapter 3

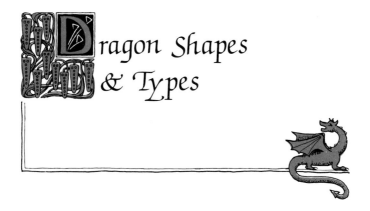

ragon Shapes & Types

Having looked at the historic remains of dragon-lore, there remain many carvings and symbols depicted on ancient artefacts which are remnants of pre-Christian religions, and which may throw more light on the subject of the dragon.

Looking for dragon remains, we find many still left in church carvings, and in such things as mazes and croziers. These, with their intricate medieval symbolism, and linked to other features in our landscape such as hill-forts and spiral mounds, hint at a lost dragon tradition which has never been written down, but which has nevertheless been understood and used by country people and even the Christian Church, which took over many pagan sites and customs in the name of Christianity.

The dragon, although it has so many meanings, seems to basically symbolise energy and can be loosely classified in the same categories as the basic elements: the natural fertile energy of the earth can be seen in the Earth

Mother religion; the sky or aerial dragon can be seen in electrical energy; water dragons live in seas and lakes; and fire dragons are symbolised by the salamander.

Fire Dragons

The salamander as a symbol rather than the living reptile, can be found both in alchemy and mythology as a small dragon which lives in fire. The Romans believed asbestos to be the wool of the salamander because it protected from heat so well. The symbol is widely used in alchemical texts, as it was believed to be an animal so cold, that it could put out a fire.

Benvenito Cellini, goldsmith, sculptor and alchemist, tells in his autobiography how, when he was a small boy, he saw a lizard-like creature in the flames of the fire in his home. He told his father, who said it was a salamander, and who then beat him - to make sure that he would remember it.

Water Dragons

We have already looked briefly at sea dragons (pg. 6) and the Anglo-Saxon 'nicor'. In *The Evolution of the Dragon*, G. Elliott Smith makes a good case for the early dragons symbolising water and early irrigation systems. "The original dragon", he says "was a benificent creature, the personification of water, and was identified with kings and gods."

"The fundamental element in the dragon's powers is the control of water. Both in its benificent and destructive aspects water was regarded as animated by the dragon", who could take on the role of Osiris or his enemy Set. But attributes of the Water God became confused with those of the Great Mother, and her darker form, the lioness (Sekhet) in Egypt, and the destructive former great Goddess Tiamat in Babylonia. They became the symbol of disorder and chaos, and the dragon became identified with them also.

He believed the earliest representation of a dragon to be a compound of an eagle and a lion, found on an archaic cylinder seal from Susa.

The dragon is also found in South America, amongst the Mayans. Here he could be either the enemy of the rain god Chac, bottling up the rain and preventing it from reaching the earth, or his helper, conserving the water ready to release it.

Earth Dragons

The symbol of the earth dragon most commonly used is that of the spiral, and this can be seen in many things such as mazes, coiled Nagas in India, prehistoric camps and spiralled or terraced hills in Britain.

Of the sixty or so dragon legends I have found so far, over half the dragons

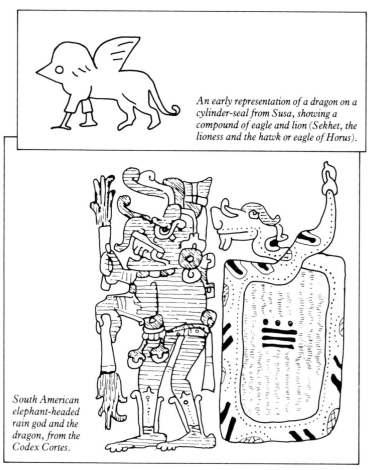

An early representation of a dragon on a cylinder-seal from Susa, showing a compound of eagle and lion (Sekhet, the lioness and the hawk or eagle of Horus).

South American elephant-headed rain god and the dragon, from the Codex Cortes.

are connected with hills, and many dragons coil themselves round those hills. In the legend of the Linton dragon, for example, the dragon in its dying moments coiled round its hill - Wormington Hill - and contracted, squeezing the hill into its spiral form. A similar thing is reputed to have happened at Bignor Hill in Sussex. These stories may be a symbolic way of describing how some mounds were re-shaped, probably for religious reasons, or for some use in that religion, perhaps for storing or controlling some sort of static electrical current, in a similar way that stone circles may have been used. One can feel this current sometimes at sacred sites and churches, variously described as a tingling sensation in the fingers, in the spine or back of the neck. Or it can be a sense of great peace, or just a strange feeling about a place. Whatever this energy really is, it is very strong when concentrated - strong enough, so legend has it, that when the dragon's blood is spilled - or when something goes wrong with the energy - no grass will grow on the site. This is said to have happened at Dragon Hill, just below the White Horse at Uffington in Berkshire. This is one of the traditional places at which St. George is supposed to have killed the dragon, and there remains on top of the mound a patch of open chalk. The same thing is reputed to have happened at the place where John Hext killed a dragon near Aller in Somerset.

The possible shaping of hills could be a British version of the Chinese form of geomancy, or Feng-shui, practised in China before the revolution. Literally translated, feng-shui means wind/water, because like wind you cannot comprehend it, and like water you cannot grasp it. The term refers to the natural science of creating harmony in the landscape, even to the extent of levelling the top of a hill if a better balance could be attained. Before building a house, the geomancers would be called in to find the location with the best 'feeling'. The Chinese believed that there were two main forces to balance this system: the mountains, symbolised by the azure dragon; and the plains symbolised by the white tiger. To them the dragon is traceable in the outlines of hills or mountains, and sometimes the backbone of the dragon can be seen along a ridge of hills, with his heart on one of the highest. From this run the 'lung mei' or dragon lines, unseen lines of natural energy. Only the Chinese royal families were allowed to have their tombs placed on the more important of these lines. Stephen Feuchtwang, in his book *Chinese Geomancy*, writes of the emphasis on the importance of shape to control the 'dragon's breath' in the landscape.

In Britain we see it in the building of mounds and 'camps' on hills, and it is later continued by the Church's policy of building churches dedicated to St. Michael the dragon-killer over possible old sites on hilltops and other high, unlikely places. In some parts of the country, Wiltshire and Somerset for example, many of the hills have prehistoric earthworks on them. Some may have been fortified camps, or terraces on which to grow crops above the flood-plane, but there are so many, that they cannot all have been so. It has been calculated that many of these camps were too large to be defensible as forts at the time they were built.

It is more likely that they have a religious significance. Dragons are sometimes associated with the camps, implying a link. The Vurm of Shervage Wood used to lie around "in and out of the trees an' round about the camp, so big and fat round as two-three girt oaks".

The spiral form is seen in other prehistoric earthworks such as mazes, and hills with possible ceremonial ridges cut into them can be found at Glastonbury and Burrowbridge, both in Somerset, and both with St. Michael churches on the top. The spiral may also be important to another part of the Earth-Mother mysteries: that of rebirth and initiation ceremonies. The treading of the maze or ceremonial path would work in a similar way to entering a labyrinth or subterranean chambers used in other parts of the world for this purpose. The idea was that one should go back into the Mother or the Earth, or work ones way towards the centre, face ordeals and meet oneself mentally and spiritually, so that one would emerge as a fully individuated

a   *b*   *c*

d   *e*

Various shapes of earth dragons: a) a maze formerly at Rockcliffe Marsh, Cumberland; b) a maze from the church of St. Adriano in Rome (6th-12th century AD); c) a 16th century map detail; d) a ridged hill: the back of Glastonbury Tor, around which there may have been a ceremonial processional path; and e) the 18th century antiquarian William Stukeley's drawing of Avebury and its avenues, symbolising a solar disc and serpent.

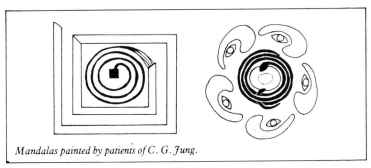

Mandalas painted by patients of C. G. Jung.

person, a theme which re-appears in modern psychology, as seen in mandalas painted by the patients of C. G. Jung.

The coiled snake, and therefore the dragon in some cases, is a major symbol for this process of self-discovery, for a number of reasons. In the ancient world, the snake was supposed to be an intermediary with the Earth-Mother because it lived in holes in the ground and it was believed to hold the secret of immortality, because of the way in which it sheds its skin and so is perpetually renewed.

Finally, because of the way in which a snake regurgitates the remains of food it does not want, it is also a very old and widespread symbol of rebirth. The symbol was used in this way in ancient Greece (pg. 7), where the snake developed, in this particular aspect, into the dragon. There are many depictions throughout the world of the dragon swallowing and regurgitating people, one of its most common usages being in Judaism and Christianity. They are identifiable as dragons rather than snakes because they have ears, and many also acquire upturned snouts.

Take, for instance, the Old Testament story of Jonah and the Big Fish. The Bible does not call the 'fish' a 'whale', and early depictions of the story show

Jonah and the Fish, from a 4th century lipsanoteca.

the fish as a curly sea serpent or dragon. Jonah emerged from the fish renewed, having overcome his doubts and fears. Jewish rabbinical tradition tells that when Jonah was swallowed by the fish, he saw 'mighty mysteries' there.

According to the Medieval 'Theory of Types', in which it was believed that each story in the New Testament had a parallel story in the Old Testament, Jonah and his ordeal in the fish was paralleled with the crucifixion and resurrection of Jesus Christ, the most important rebirth in the Christian world. This theme is found in church symbolism, on artefacts such as croziers.

A medieval crozier from the Britsh Museum symbolising the Resurrection of the Lamb, Jesus Christ.

Detail from a 9th century ivory relief of the Crucifixion, used for the cover of Henry II's Book of Pericopes, early 11th century.

A similar image is found in the dark age tradition of portraying the Crucifixion with a dragon coiled round its base. There was a 9th century school of ivory carving which specialised in these Crucifixion scenes with dragons on. At first glance it might appear that carvings such as this are a conventional reference to Christ's victory over death and the Devil. But the dragon does not look beaten or cast down. It is the earth dragon who waits. Many allusions to the old religion can be found in sculpture at this time, with Christian stories entwined with pagan ones. A good example of this can be seen on the 8th century Ruthwell Cross in Dumfriesshire, where there is a runic poem telling the story of the crucifixion, together with embellishments from the death of Baldur the Beautiful, the Norse Year-King.

There was a dragon coiled round the world tree in Norse mythology: the Nidhogg was coiled round the root of the great ash tree, Yggdrasil, which supported the world, and was slowly devouring it.

Another type of energy connected with the earth and ancient sites is to see the dragon as a barrow-guardian. That dragons guarded treasure hords was their main attribute according to the Anglo-Saxons, and they called burial mounds 'dragon hills'. The dragon that finally killed Beowulf was the guardian of a long-barrow, who went on the rampage after a cup had been stolen from his hord, whilst in the Mabinogian, in the romance of Peredur, son of Efrawg, reference is made to a barrow in Wales, guarded by a Worm. These stories may refer to spiritual treasures, or the knowledge of earth energy hidden inside barrows. But there was also a strongly held belief that the mounds contained real treasure. In most cases this has proved completely erroneous. Silbury Hill in Wiltshire, amongst others, was supposed to contain a horse and rider covered with gold. Nothing of any material value has ever - as far as we know - been found in it.

The Norse Sutton Hoo burial mound proved different, many beautiful items have been discovered in the long-boat burial there.

There is also another strange British legend about a dragon guarding treasure at Bromfield in Shropshire, supposed to have taken place in 1344. The dragon was killed by a Saracen physician, and afterwards some local men went to see if there was any treasure there. There was, but the landowner, Earl Warren imprisoned them and kept it for himself.

Aerial Dragons

This type of dragon has a more linear shape, and his elaborate coils symbolise the energising and electrical nature of the form. The constant movement of this dragon was best portrayed by the Danish Ringerike style of carving, although we can see it depicted in earlier forms too.

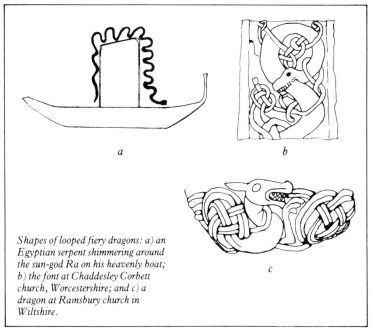

Shapes of looped fiery dragons: a) an Egyptian serpent shimmering around the sun-god Ra on his heavenly boat; b) the font at Chaddesley Corbett church, Worcestershire; and c) a dragon at Ramsbury church in Wiltshire.

The twisting shapes are powerful images of energy: as one looks at them they seem to move. They are similar to something I saw some years ago, whilst riding a cycle one morning down an ordinary street in London. I saw above one of the houses a bright object, a ball of fire, within which were writhing gold 'serpents'. There was no real pattern to them; the closest analogy I can think of is as though a quantity of thick string had been dropped so that the loops of string formed a random heap. As I watched, these loops writhed, although I must have seen it for only a few seconds. Looking back up the road I could see nothing. Although most people will probably think it was a 'flight of the imagination', it was quite real to me - and very puzzling. I do not take hallucinatory drugs and never have done, so it cannot have been due to that either. Some colleagues have suggested that what I saw was what is known to mystics as an elemental or 'deva', a natural energy form which is not usually visible, and may account for what some people see as UFOs, or ghosts. It may have been some form of ball lighning, as it appeared to be hovering over a lightning conductor on the house. It had no three dimensional form as I could see it, it was just a set of loops of a very bright pale gold.

Motif taken from a buckle found at Sutton Hoo.

Several years later, when researching the subject of dragons, and looking at the various pictorial forms, it occurred to me that if I wished to portray this writhing energy, the drawing would be similar to an elaborately coiled Ringerike dragon-carving. The illustration, taken from a buckle found in the Sutton Hoo burial is an almost exact representation of what I saw, except that I did not see any heads on it.

So here may be another type of dragon, which may have a semi-physical reality. If I can see these things, then I am sure other people can see them too - perhaps the elaborate ringerike dragons are how the Saxons and Danes saw and portrayed them too. The Danes carved their boat prows with ornate and fearsome dragon heads. That they believed them to be powerful elemental forces is shown in the practice of the heads being detachable, so that when they returned home, they were taken down so as not to frighten the 'landvettir', the local, peaceful countryside spirits.

It also brings us back to the question of the archetype and the externalised symbol, for if people in the past interpreted such phenomena as dragons rather than UFOs, which they tend to explain these things as now, this may be the nearerst we are ever going to get to the 'physical' dragon.

Ball lightning has tended to behave in odd ways too, with sightings reported in the papers from time to time. I remember a case some years ago of a ball of blue-white light moving up the isle of a passenger aircraft before disappearing through the plane's side, whilst it was flying through a thunderstorm.

Later depictions of dragons, painted or carved in the Middle Ages when the ringerike style had passed out of fashion, still indicate energy by having looped tails. Most Christian or Church dragons have at least one loop in their tales.

Many flying dragons are found in legends. In some cases, dragons are believed to fly or travel along a line between ancient sites - unfortunately being so predictable caused them to be ambushed by several of the heroes in dragon legends. In the story of the Aller dragon for instance, the fiery dragon used to fly across the marshes from Curry Rivel, for about three miles, in a straight line.

There may be a link here with the theory of ley-lines. Alfred Watkins' term 'ley lines' originally applied to the alignment of ancient sites such as St. Michael churches with their dragon connections, and prehistoric mounds and stone circles. John Michell, in his book *View Over Atlantis* writes of a large ley-type line he has found which connects mainly St. Michael or other dragon sites. It starts at Ogbourne St. George in Wiltshire, runs through Avebury, St. Michael's church on Glastonbury Tor, St. Michael's church on Burrowbridge Mump, and on through several other sites in Somerset and Devon to St. Michael's Mount in Cornwall. Strong evidence that these lines do carry some kind of energy or force is continually being put forward by physicists and dowsers alike, and no doubt that at some time in the future will be 'scientifically proved'.

Dragons also link sites in a smaller area, which in time became named after them. Often the dragon lived on a certain hill (such as a Worm Hill or Drakelow), came down to drink at a certain well or at the river. It seems that most of the sacred sites in an area would be linked by the dragon - perhaps symbolising a local energy current - which would move between them, although not necessarily in a straight line, but more as an energy area.

An example of a probable smaller-scale site alignment is the story of the Long, Long Worm, collected from a gypsy near what is now the Watford/Elstree by-pass. This dragon was one of the wingless fire-breathing type who lay on or near a lane which was an ancient trackway to the local fair, some way off. It also lay over some treasure (the remains of a barrow mound?) and was killed by the gypsies for this reason. Here is a case of the dragon almost being the alignment, and perhaps his buried body was a symbol of the path between the sites.

One wonders whether electrical energy or something similar such as orgone energy is stored in burial mounds. Several old accounts of the opening of barrows tell of the strange and violent thunderstorms which occur soon afterwards. If the dragon, legendary burial mound guardian, was linked in peoples' minds with this sort of terrifying phenomenon, no wonder that the dragon remained a very powerful image. The dragon at Longwitton in Yorkshire, for instance, is recorded as having been able to change into a whirlwind, a similar phenomenon to the tornado which struck the house of the plunderer of a cairn at Torrylin, Arran. L. V. Grinsell in *Folklore of Prehistoric Sites in Britain* also tells of a mysterious light which travelled between a cairn at Torhousetie (Wigtownshire) and a water conduit which had been covered by a slab taken from it.

Paul Devereux, in his book *Earth Lights* (Turnstone, 1982) makes an interesting correlation between ball lightning and UFOs, and their frequency in being recorded at ancient sites. Are these, perhaps, a more modern version of the dragons once seen? These phenomena also seem to have a link with fault lines and areas of geological instability.

Chapter 4

British Dragon Legends

There are many dragon legends spread over the British Isles. All that remains of many of them is that a dragon appeared and was killed by a local hero, with virtually no other information. Quite often there is a 'Worm Hill' or some other local feature named after a dragon. Although one or two places are pointed out as being the spot where 'St. George killed the dragon' there appears to be no legend of his actually killing a specific dragon in Britain. Some of the stories could be allegorical, relating to pests of the human kind, while in others the dragon is revealed by other sources to be a large but common animal.

The Pollard Worm at Bishop Auckland in Durham appears to belong to this latter group. The champion who killed the beast was Pollard of Pollard Hall. His reward was as much land as he could ride round while the Bishop dined. Unfortunately another source refers not to a dragon which was responsible for terrorising the local countryside, but a large boar.

Different versions appear of the great Linton Worm, who was able to coil himself round Worm Hill three times. As a reward for killing the beast, Somerville was given the title of Kings Falconer in 1174 for his brave deed, and the Somerville family still own some of the land granted to him at the time. The Somerville coat of arms shows a crested dragon. However, in the 'Memoirs of the Somervilles', published in 1680, the great dragon is described as "in length three Scots yards, and somewhat bigger than an ordinary man's leg, with a head more proportionable to its length than greatness, in form and colour like our common muir-edders".

A stone sculptured relief of the hero plunging his lance down the throat of one of two creatures, with a lamb behind him, can be found in Linton church. Beneath it, now defaced, is an inscription which is believed to have read:

> The wode Laird of Larristone
> Slew the Worm of Wormestone
> And wan a' Linton parochine.

Some sceptical people say that it was the carving that gave rise to the legend.

So this dragon may have been just a large eel, although that does not explain everything, for there is certainly something 'dragonish' in the area. There is the coiled Wormington Hill or Wormestone, which according to the legend received its ridges directly from the coils of the dragon, a "Worms Hole" in a hollow on Linton Hill, and the old carving.

The Somerville family must have been famed for dragon-killing as the name also appears in Somerset, at the village of Dinder near Wells, where a St. Michael church stands on a pre-historic mound, and the local pub, now closed, was called "The Dragon on the Wheel", another Somerville coat of arms. A mile away is the hamlet of Worminster, and a nearby hill has a notch cut round the top of it.

Some dragons have been well documented, and seen by many people. The dragon of Wantley in Lancashire, for instance, had a pamphlet written about him in 1614. This dragon had 44 iron teeth, a long sting in his tail, and wings. He breathed fire and ate children. More of More Hall was the knight who agreed to fight it. He equipped himself with a suit of armour with large spikes on and hid in a well where the dragon used to drink. The fight lasted for two days until More was able to drive an iron spike into the middle of its back and kill it. Do we at last we have a well authenticated and well documented story of a dragon killing? Unfortunately not so. There is a theory that the whole episode is a veiled account of how a wicked landlord was thwarted in his plans to evict his tenants by a clever lawyer named More, although there are some very strange old traditions in it.

The Henham dragon was also well documented, and in this case there is

The Wantley Dragon.

nothing to suspect him of being a boar or a human. A pamphlet entitled *The Flying Serpent, or Strange News out of Essex*, was published about him in 1669. He was about nine feet long, had small wings and curious eyes with what looked like feathers radiating from them, rather like an owl's. His tail was pointed like an arrowhead, and a short arrow as well as a tongue projected from a well-fanged mouth. The pamphlet was probably written by a Robert Winstanly, who published *Poor Robin's Almanack*. Repeated appearances were recorded, and in 1674 there was an announcement for a fair to be held at Henham, for the sale of 'Flying Serpents'!

Of the many dragon legends in the country, there are several aspects which it is interesting to look at, such as the type of hero to kill the dragon, different attributes of the dragons and how the heroes tackled these various difficulties.

The dragon heroes were drawn from a wide range of ordinary people. Often the dragon-killer was a local lad who made his name and fortune by his deed. At Arundel, Jim Pulk was a farmer's son, at Deehurst; John Smith was a labourer, while at Mordiford a condemened criminal named Garston was sent out redeem himself, and won his freedom and some land in return for killing the beast.

At Shervage Wood in the Quantocks the dragon-slayer was a woodman, who, looking for faggots and knowing nothing of the 'vurm' there, sat to eat his lunch on what he thought was a log. The vurm, which was the log, squirmed, and jumping up, the woodman cut it in two with his axe. One half of the dragon is said to have run to Bilbrook, and the other half to Kingston St. Mary.

Sometimes a local knight was responsible for the downfall of the dragon. In 1405 at Bures in Essex, the local lord Sir Richard de Waldegrave organised other local men in an archery attack and drove it into a marsh.

On other occasions the villagers hired a soldier of fortune to kill the beast for them. At Bisterne, Sir Maurice Berkeley was hired for the task, and although he fulfilled it, he died soon afterwards. At the castle of Caledfryn-yn-Rhos, now Denbigh, in Wales, a member of the Salisbury family of Lleweni took on the job. Known as Sir John of the Thumbs, because he had eight fingers and two thumbs on each hand, he fought the dragon and cut off its head. He shouted 'Dym bych' - or 'no more dragon' as he returned with the head, which, according to Henderson's *Folklore of the Northern Counties and Borders* is where the name of Denbigh came from.

At Lambton, the young lord may have been the cause, and was the cure for the dragon there. As a youth he fished up a worm so ugly, that he swore when he saw it and threw it down a well. In the course of time he became a knight, joined the crusades and was absent for many years. He returned to find that the worm had grown into a dragon which was responsible or eating several people a day, and so undertook to kill the beast.

One of the most unusual dragon-killers must be the Saracen physician who killed the dragon at a mound at Bromfield in 1344, by using incantations.

Men - and women - of God have also taken part in several legends of dragon-killing as well as St. George and St. Michael.

Bishop Jocelyn of Wells killed a dragon which had swallowed some children, and when he cut the dragon open the children jumped out.

A couple of dragon legends are connected with Winlatter Rock near Chesterfield, and one concerns a missionary Priest, who, seeing the Devil come from the North in the form of a fiery dragon, jumped on to the rock and spread his arms wide to form a cross. The devil sent three tempests to blow the Priest off, but the latter stood so firm that his feet sank into the rock and held him up, and the Devil retreated. Apparently Winlatter Rock is still there, but weather and frost broke off the piece with the Priest's footmarks in many years ago.

It is among the Christian saints that we meet two lady dragon-heroines, St. Martha and St. Margaret.

According to the Auchinleck manuscript, St. Margaret was swallowed by a dragon which then burst open, and she was able to step out unharmed. In another legend, as a Christian, she had to endure several ordeals, one of which included being bound and placed in a tank of water, from which she escaped unharmed. She is sometimes depicted with a fish tail to symbolise her power over water.

St. Martha was a French saint who came from the cathedral at Aix-en-Provence to subdue the local dragon, the Tarasque, which she did by sprinkling it with holy water and holding a crucifix before it. When the dragon became docile, people pulled hairs out of its tail, believing that they would gain its strength.

The Tarasque, a French dragon which inhabited the area around Aix-en-Provence.

The Norse hero and dragon slayer Siegfried is said to have appropriated the dragon's strength by eating its heart. It also gave him the ability to understand the language of animals.

There are many obscure localised dragon-saints. In the 6th century, St. Leonard near Horsham in Sussex, drove a dragon deeper and deeper into the forest where 'it was thought to be slain'.

The strange early legend of St. Carantacus tells how he threw a 'massy altar' into the River Severn, and vowed to build a church where it landed. King Arthur found it while on his way to kill a dragon at Dunster, and, later, meeting the Saint a few miles away, asked him to prove who he was by raising the dragon. Carantacus spoke to the marshes (Carr or Carhampton Marshes near Dunster) and the dragon rose up and crawled to the Saint, who tied his shawl around its neck. Arthur granted him twelve portions of land on which to build his church, but took the 'massy altar'' to build the Round Table.

Heroes have often had to be quite ingenious in the way that they have killed their dragons, the main problem being that dragons are often said to have had poisonous or fiery breath. Other dragons have been supposedly able to join themselves up again after being cut to pieces, and several heroes overcame this problem by having knives fixed to their armour, which continued to cut the dragon, and by having dogs to carry the dragon pieces away before they had time to re-heal.

The dragon's fiery breath appears in various forms in virtually all dragon legends, and is worth investigating more closely. There may be a link here with the earth energies discussed earlier. On page 22 we looked at *feng shui*. In his book ***Chinese Geomancy*** Stephen Feuchtwang writes of the Chinese emphasis on the importance of shape to control the 'dragon's breath' in the landscape. He also talks of 'sha' or 'noxious breath', and this could be an explanation for the poisonous dragon's breath in the British legends. By comparison, and from Feuchtwang's description of it, it seems to correspond to the 'black radiations' that European dowsers have dealt with for the past fifty years or so. These 'black radiations' can be found directly above certain underground water-bearing fissures or 'black streams', and affect the health of people, animals and crops above them as a result of an energy imbalance somewhere in the earth. The usual way that dowsers deal with these 'black streams' is to stake them - as a practitioner in acupuncture would 'stake' a node on an acupuncture meridian to restore balance in the human body. We have already seen examples of the earth dragon being symbolically staked in fertility and earth-stimulating celebrations. In legend dragons are often speared, with a weapon usually of iron, such as an iron-tipped spear. Iron stakes are used in the acupuncture of the earth in order to restore its balance.

An example of earth-acupuncture of this kind took place in a small religious community in the Cotswolds a few years ago. Before it was done, the valley was dead, and very little would grow there. The 'life' was restored to it by staking the ground with iron stakes at certain points in the valley chosen by a dowser. The balance of the land had apparently been upset by quarrying work a few miles away. Perhaps this is what was meant by the 'poisonous breath' of the dragon, which people were so afraid of - an imbalance of some kind which would ruin their crops and their livelihood.

The dowser in this case was a follower of Zoroaster, and he told me that dragons are regarded in that religion as evil things in the earth, imbalances that need to be rebalanced. Taken generally, the dragon is not of itself evil, it only becomes evil when the energy it represents is out of control or not properly balanced. In Chinese terms, Yin and Yang would be out of balance, and the dragon's blood and breath would have turned sour, into 'noxious breath'.

So perhaps dragon-killing and dragon-taming legends could be seen as stories of the controlling or re-balancing of these earth energies. In China and Persia the dragon has long had an association of this kind - here is a possible British equivalent. A local hero may have set the balance right by 'staking the dragon' - perhaps the chalk hill figure of the Long Man of Wilmington represents such a hero, as he stands with his two spears or poles.

Unfortunately, even though they took measures to protect themselves,

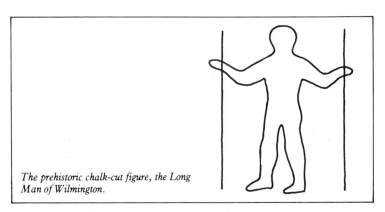

The prehistoric chalk-cut figure, the Long Man of Wilmington.

several of the heroes died afterwards from the effects of the 'noxious breath' they had to deal with.

The Yorkshire story of Peter Loschy is one such example. Peter covered his armour with razor blades so that the dragon would not crush him, and as he cut pieces off the dragon, his dog carried them away to a hill near Nunnington church, beginning with the tail and ending with the head. This could be symbolic of the way in which the bad energy was broken down and transferred to a possible sacred site which could absorb it. Both Peter and his dog died afterwards from the poison they had absorbed.

John Hext, when he was about to meet the dragon near Aller, had a long spear made - with an iron tip - so that he might escape the dragon's fiery breath. Unfortunately it did not work - he killed the dragon but was burned to death in the process. The spear he is said to have used is still kept in a nearby church in Somerset.

Sir Maurice Berkely at Bisterne in Hampshire tried to protect himself by plastering his body with bird-lime, then sprinkling it with powered glass - but that did not save him either. Perhaps he should have used crystal glass, like the knight who killed a cockatrice near Saffon Walden in Essex. Quartz crystal, the basic substance of crystal glass, is a refractor and polariser of light-energy, and probably earth-energy too, as it is a chief component of many standing stones. Perhaps it contains some element of importance to the control of those energies.

There are the remains of old magic in the story of the Wantley dragon. According to the pamphlet on the subject, the dragon was still alive at the time it was written, in about 1614, and as we have seen, may be suspect. However there is another version of the story from *Legends and Traditions of Lancaster* by Harland and Wilkinson. The knight who agreed to fight it was also named as More of More Hall - a strange man who sounds more like a pre-Christian supernatural hero than a medieval knight (and even less like a lawyer). It was said that he had once killed a horse which had angered him by seizing its main and tail and swinging it round and round until it died. Then he ate it - all except the head.

More had a suit of armour made with five inch spikes on, and he requested that a black-haired maiden of sixteen should anoint him the night before the battle, and arm him in the morning. For two days More and the dragon fought, and on the third day he succeeded in driving an iron stake into the 'vital spot' on the dragon's back. The dragon spun round and round, and died within a few minutes.

The last story involving the use of very powerful 'electrical' forces is that of the Three Valiant Lads, the second of the legends about Winlatter Rock, as told in Ruth Tongue's book *Forgotten Folk Tales*. These are the only British legend I have found in which the dragon is actually supposed to be the Devil. The dragon came from the North, burning the land as he came. Three boys had a huge iron sword made, which they stood in a socket on top of Winlatter Rock (perhaps one of the Priest's footmarks?). When the dragon appeared, they spun the sword round and round. At this the dragon raised a thunderstorm, and the lightning flashing from the sword was the signal that the people of Chesterfield and Grindleford should ring their church bells. At this, the dragon fled down the Blue John mine.

This remarkable story involves the linking of sites and the use of powerful aerial electrical energies triggered by an iron implement. Most of Winlatter Rock must have crumbled away, for there is no trace of it on a map, although there is an Eagle Rock up in that area, with a set of legends of its own. Still, it is interesting that so many clues to the controlling of powerful earth energies should exist in one story - however true, untrue or wrongly placed it it may be.

Chapter 5

Saint George & Saint Michael

St. George became the champion of England just after the first Crusade to the Holy Land in 1099, when the crusaders brought him back as a warrior saint, having discovered his tomb in Palestine. In spite of the many stories which grew up around him, virtually nothing is known about his life, although it is believed that he was martyred for his faith around 300 AD.

Several gospels were written about him, the earliest being that supposedly written by his manservant Pasicrates, and translated by Sir E. A. Wallis Budge from Coptic and Arabic texts, *St. George of Lydda: Ethiopic Texts and Translations*. The earliest of these dates from the 6th century, and tells of George's martyrdom at the hands of a Persian king, Dâdhyânos (although there is no record of a king of that name). There is no mention of a dragon, although in an early part of the Coptic narrative, Dâdhyânos is described as a Gevya Garsa - a serpent viper - and that seems to be the closest St. George ever came to a dragon.

Another reference to St. George comes from the historian Gelasius of Caesarea, writing in 385 AD. He lists St. George among early Christians martyred on the orders of the Roman Emperor Diocletian. So the whole of George's story is muddled to say the least. The two accounts seem to be of two different people. Sometimes he is called George of Cappadocia, but according to others this is not the true George either. At one stage he was even mistaken for a heretical Arian bishop of Alexandria, and so many versions of his life were appearing, that in 494 Pope Gelasius issued a warning to the Catholic Church against believing in certain 'forged and false acts of St. George'.

According to the Roman version of the story, a tomb was built for him at his birthplace, Lydda, in Palestine, which gained a reputation for healing. He was a well-known saint long before the first Crusade of 1099 - he is referred to by the early English historian Bede (673-735).

The European crusaders came upon St. George's tomb at a depressing time in their campaign. They decided to try his patronage, won the next battle, (that of Acre), and also saw what they believed to be the knight himself fighting among them. After that, they adopted him as their martial saint, and brought him back to England where he replaced St. Edward the Confessor as the country's patron saint.

So where then, is the dragon, which according to Caxton's *Golden Legend* of 1483 needed four carts to carry its remains out of the city?

A few miles away from the tomb at Lydda, is Joppa, legendary site of the battle between the Greek hero Perseus and a sea dragon which had come to take the maiden Andromeda. The people on the crusades probably heard this story and associated the hero with George.

George's story is that during his travels he came upon a princess, usually called Sadra, who had been left as an offering to a dragon which was devastating the countryside. Several other people and sheep had already been sacrificed, and it was her name that was pulled out when the lots were cast to find the next victim. George fought and speared the dragon, then he put the princess' girdle round its neck and led it back to the city, where he converted the people to Christianity and finally killed the beast.

In the Greek legend, Andromeda was offered as a sacrifice after her mother had boasted that her beauty was greater than that of the sea nymphs. These became jealous and persuaded Poseidon, god of the sea to send a dragon to destroy the town. Andromeda was chained to a rock outside the town as an offering to the dragon and to placate Poseidon. She was saved by Perseus, who, like George, happened to be travelling by and saw her.

They are similar stories, although each a product of the beliefs of the culture to which they belong - one a pagan squabble between humans and spirits or

*St. George, from a late
14th century Russian
painting in the
Novgorodian style.*

wrathful gods, the other the monotheistic Christian battle between good and evil - a useful adaptation from the former story, and it is easy to see how they could have become confused.

George's fame spread very quickly in England once the crusaders brought him back. He was famous primarily as a martial saint, but he also seems to have taken on the characteristics of an older, Celtic dragon-killing god. Further weight would be given to this belief as his name was translated from the Greek meaning 'tiller of the earth' and he could be identified with old gods who were responsible for waking up the earth after Winter. John Michell in *View Over Atlantis* suggests that George took over the attributes of the Celtic solar god Og or Ock, as their names coincide at a number of places, Ogbourne St. George for example.

Other legends have grown up around St. George. Alice Brewster wrote a small book about the legend for Boy Scouts in 1914, which includes many wonderful stories about him, including that he was a friend of the first Christian Roman Emperor Constantine, and came with him to England.

They visited Constantine's mother, Queen Helena of York, and also Glastonbury, where he came to see the tomb of Joseph of Arimathea "said to be one of his ancestors". Alice Brewster believed that the dragon was a crocodile, and used George's fight as a lesson to us to stand up and overcome things we have to, and not to "shirk duty".

The first dragon-killer in Britain was the Archangel St. Michael, because of the part he took in the killing of the dragon in the Book of Revelations. St. George was a useful hero to take over St. Michael's role on Earth, as he was a figure who could be more easily related to by the people - except perhaps in Cornwall, where St. Michael is very popular. St. Michael was the stern avenger of God, who conquered Satan and who was rather a forbidding figure.

A tympanum from the church at Moreton Valence, Gloucestershire, c. 1120.

Many of the carvings of dragon-killers in this country are of St. Michael, usually shown spearing a dragon. There is a very interesting piece in *English Romanesque Sculpture, 1066-1140* by the art historian George Zarnecki, where he compares the French and English schools of carving at that period. He chooses a French St. Michael carving, and compares it with an English one, from the tympanum over the doorway of St. Stephen's church at Moreton Valence in Gloucestershire, from around 1120. He describes the British one as being more harmonious, like a ritual or a dance. He describes it as having a "feeling of almost lyrical serenity", and it is treated more decoratively compared with the French one, which depicts an active battle. Did the person who carved the British one have a dance or ritual in mind when he carved it?

In other places the dragon carvings are not so graceful. There is an interesting one carved on the font at Avebury in Wiltshire. Although it is now quite worn, one can make out the figure of what looks like a bishop, striking a dragon with his crozier. However the dragon is not quite dead, for he appears to be biting the man's foot. It is a significant find in a place of such old-religion power as Avebury, so close to the huge stone circle there, and may show the battle the Christian priests had with the old religion. Sometimes the dragons reach frightening proportions, as with the three headed monster carved on the

Above: Detail from the font at Avebury, Wiltshire.

Right: The font at Thorpe Arnold church, Leicestershire.

font at Thorpe Arnold church.

At other times dragons are shown on their own, without a dragon killer. Sometimes these are purely for decoration or as gargoyles and water spouts. Sometimes, particularly when just one dragon is depicted, they are a

*The intricate dragon from
the font of Chaddesley
Corbett church, c. 1160.*

*Dragon on a tympanum at
Uppington, Shropshire,
late 11th century.*

reminder of the old religion, set into the fabric of the church in a similar way to
the carvings of the 'Green Man' and other pre-Christian images found in
churches throughout the country.

Chapter 6

King Arthur & the use of the Dragon in Heraldry

Arthur and his knights of the Round Table are supposed to have killed many dragons in the course of their adventures, and Geoffrey of Monmouth, from whom many of these legends come, says that Arthur wore a 'helm of gold graven with the semblance of a dragon'. Yet in reality, virtually nothing is known about the man. A local tribal leader called Arthur is mentioned in the Welsh Barddas which gives the impression that he was little more than a rather lecherous, glorified pig-thief.

According to legend, Arthur's father was Uther Pendragon: Pendragon meaning the 'head of the dragon' which in heraldic usage stands for courage, wisdom and leadership. At that time the dragon was a respected image for use in battle. The Romans used it as a badge for a cohort - and this is where the connection with the historical person called Arthur lies.

In around 400 AD when the main armies of Rome left Britain, defence and leadership of the country was placed in the hands of a 'dux bellorum', a

Romano-British warlord. The name of the main dux bellorum responsible for holding back the Anglo-Saxon invasion for any length of time has been lost - but it was very probably Arthur. This man became the basis for many legends, and as with St. George he gathered many attributes of both a Christian and a pre-Christian nature.

The dragon's place in this is found in the dragon pennons which Arthur would have flown above his army, after the fashion of the Roman cohorts. As Arthur and his men were gradually pushed back into Wales, the red dragon standard became the symbol of the Celt, or the Romano-British spirit fighting the Saxon, and in time became the symbol of Wales.

A Carolingian soldier using a dragon pennant, from the Psalterium Aureum, 841-872.

The red dragon or 'Y ddraig Coch' has often been of particular importance to Wales and its identity. Great things were expected of Prince Machynlleth whose birth was marked by the appearance of a comet shaped like a red dragon, in 1402. It is only recently, however, that it has been the official badge of Wales. The Prince of Wales has had a dragon on his shield since 1911 when it was decreed by George V, and it was not until 1953 that Queen Elizabeth II made it the official Welsh flag.

The historical Arthurian explanation of the red dragon as the symbol for Wales is more likely than the legendary one, which is usually assumed to account for it. This version involves a boy, variously named as Myrrdin or Ambrosius - the Merlin of Geoffrey of Monmouth - who, on account of his being a 'boy without a father' was chosen as a sacrifice by the magicians of

King Vortigern to placate the spirits at a place where he wished to build a castle, but where the earth kept moving and destroying the foundations (now Beddgelert in North Wales). The boy spoke up and prophesied that the real cause of the tremors was that two dragons were fighting beneath the site, and that it was a omen concerning the war against the English. So Vortigern had a pit dug and found the two dragons. As they watched, the red dragon won against the white. The red dragon stood for Wales, Merlin said, and the white for the English. Vortigern was so pleased with this that he made Merlin his court magician in place of the previous false advisers.

The dragon was a popular military symbol, for in time the Anglo-Saxons adopted it. They used it at the Battle of Burford in 752, and it was also used at the Battle of Assigdon in 1016 between Edmund Ironside and Canute. King Harold used it as his standard at the Battle of Hastings in 1066.

Its use continued through Richard the Lionheart in the 1191 crusade, Henry III (who used it against the Welsh in 1245), to Henry VII who took the red dragon of Cadwaller as his symbol out of respect for his Welsh ancestry. It became Henry VIII's symbol, and later that of Elizabeth I who changed the

Detail from the Bayeux tapestry of the two dragon standards (one fallen) used by King Harold at the Battle of Hastings. The standards were made by cutting out the emblem and attaching it by the head to the staff.

colour from red to gold. James I replaced it with the Scottish unicorn.

Many families have the dragon as their heraldic beast. According to *The Heraldic Imagination* by Rodney Dennys (Barrie & Jenkins, 1975) 200 English families use it, and 300 European families. It was the Lancastrian crest around 1300.

The seal of the Earl of Lancaster.

In a few cases, there is a history of dragon-killing in the family. The Somerville crest commemorates a forbear who killed a dragon or two, and a branch of the Llewellyn family also uses it, after one of them killed a dragon at Unsworth in Lancashire. A table carved with the dagger that killed the dragon used to be pointed out at the Llewellyn's old manor house.

At present the dragon is a symbol for London, and seated silver dragons are set in the centre of roads leading into the City, at the boundaries. These dragons have acquired barbed tails as many heraldic dragons now have, a fashion which has come in since the reign of Elizabeth I, for her dragon had a smooth tail.

A red dragon is also the symbol for Somerset - perhaps another connection with Arthur, as his fort, Camelot, is believed to be at Queen Camel, and his remains were uncovered at Glastonbury Abbey a few miles away, in the 13th century - or so the monks of the time claimed, although it may have been a ploy to catch the medieval tourist trade, as the Abbey was in need of funds from visiting Pilgrims at the time. Apparently they uncovered two bodies, buried inside a large tree trunk, with a cross which read (in translation) 'here lies Arthur, the king, in the Isle of Avalon'.

Chapter 7

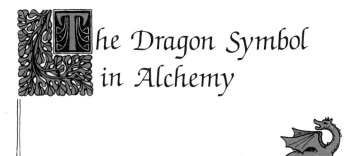

The Dragon Symbol in Alchemy

Dragons have a variety of meanings in the study of alchemy.

Sometimes the dragon represents base matter containing the seed of gold, ready to be killed and transmuted. At other times, two dragons, male and female, are shown devouring or destroying each other, and thus purifying themselves and giving rise to a 'glorified dragon', symbolising the Philosopher's Stone; or transmutation. The same symbol can also mean putrefaction. The pictorial form of this is the caduceus, the symbol of Mercury or Hermes in Roman times, and the dragon is sometimes referred to as 'Hermes Bird'.

Winged and wingless dragons symbolise the volatile and fixed principles - mercury and sulphur, and also the eternal opposites: male and female, good and evil etc. The caduceus is the symbol of the medical profession, derived from Asklepios, the Roman god of medicine, who was sometimes portrayed as a snake, and who would bite the affected part in order to heal it.

The dragon used as an emblem of the Great Work of alchemy, from the Viridarium Chymicum, Stolcius, 1624.

The caduceus from Nicolai Flamelli, Chymische Werke, Wienn, 1751.

A silver thaler. The reverse side shows Jesus being crucified.

The dragon or serpent nailed to a cross is also used, and symbolises the fixation of the volatile - part of the alchemical process. This rather odd symbol is also used in Christianity as a symbol for Jesus. It derives from a passage from the Gospel of John, Chapter 3, verse 4 where he says that Christ, like the Nehushtan or Brazen Serpent held up by Moses in the desert to save his people from a plague of serpents, must also be held up on high to save mankind.

Moses appears in connection with a serpent in another part of the Old Testament, when he and his brother Aaron had a magical battle with the Egyptian priests just before the Exodus. Moses turned his staff into a serpent, and this is portrayed in a 13th Century French enamelled cross - although it is a flying dragon which is depicted here.

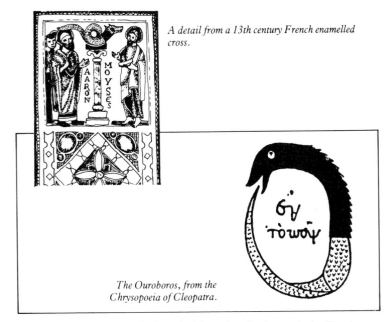

A detail from a 13th century French enamelled cross.

The Ouroboros, from the Chrysopoeia of Cleopatra.

The other main alchemical symbol featuring the dragon is the Ouroboros, the dragon or serpent which bites its own tail. This is also another symbol of purification, and more importantly the symbol of eternity, or of the universe. It first appears in ancient Egypt as far back as 1600 BC. This one is taken from the *Chrysopoeia* ('Gold Making') of Cleopatra from the Alexandrian period in Egypt, and encloses the words 'the all is one'. The black half of the body symbolises Earth and night, the white half Heaven and light. Two of the early important alchemists were women, one called Maria the Jewess, who gave her name to the *bain-marie,* and the other called Cleopatra. This was not the one who married Caesar - there were several, and the name means 'famously descended'.

The serpent with its tail in its mouth appears in other mythologies throughout the world. In Norse legend the Midgard Orm encircles the Earth. Odin tried to fish for it using a bull's head as a bait, and failed. Snorri Sturlusson, in the *Prose Edda* tells how they will meet and kill each other at the Ragnarok, the end of the World.

The symbol features in Hindu cosmology too. According to their legends, the Earth is supported on the backs of four enormous elephants, which stand on the back of a huge tortoise, which in turn is surrounded by a horizontal ouroboros - the head and tail are at the top, above the earth.

There are many other fascinating pieces of dragon-lore which I would like to include in this book but which don't fit in with the other categories.

Take, for example, the use of the dragon in dark age and medieval

An illuminated initial, showing St. Gregory, from the Morelia in Job. Painted by an English artist at Citeaux, beginning of 12th century.

illuminated manuscripts, used purely for decoration. The example here shows an initial from the *Moralia in Job*, from France, but drawn by an English artist before 1111.

The dragon is used decoratively in many contexts: this weather vane, bearing the date 1696 comes from the church of St. Mary at Latton, now part of Harlow new town.

The dragon often features in fairy stories. The Laidley Worm of Spindleston Heugh - or sometimes called the Bamborough dragon belongs more to fairy story than it does to legend. At the castle of Bamborough a wicked stepmother, who was also a witch, turned the daughter of the house into a dragon. She remained that way until the Childe of Wynde, her brother, returned to free her from the spell.

There is a French fairy story connected with the castle of Lusignan, built by magic, by Melusina, the wife of one of the dukes, who was half human, half fairy. She is portrayed in one of the monthly miniatures in the early 15th century illustrated book *Les Tres Riches Heures du Duc de Berri* as a golden dragon flying above the castle.

Some strange but interesting theories about the origin of the dragon have been put forward. Immanuel Velikovsky believes that the legends throughout the ancient world of dragon killing came from a cataclysmic happening in ancient times, when a huge comet with a long, dark, forked tail came close to the earth. The comet was drawn closer by gravitational pull and wrapped itself around the world, making the skies black. The bright head of the comet came close to its dark tail, and it appeared to the frightened people below that a star had come to combat the black, several headed monster, and so the legend of a hero fighting a dragon grew up.

Dragons in the past have tended to be regarded as evil in this country, but are now enjoying something of a comeback. They are a great favourite in children's stories, from little Welsh dragons which provide the heat to power a steam train, to a 'Listen with Mother' story I heard a couple of years ago about a dragon in Lichtenstein who had to wear dark glasses because the light hurt his eyes! Dragon processions have also taken on a new lease of life, with several being reported in towns throughout the country each summer.

So, as well as being an ancient symbol, the dragon appears to be assured of an interesting future, and is by no means dying out!

Bibliography

Chinese Geomancy, Stephen Feuchtwang (Vithagna, Laos, 1974).

Companion Into Essex, Herbert W. Tompkins (Methuen, 1938).

A Dictionary of British Folk Tales: Part B - Folk Legends Vol. 1, Katharine M. Briggs (RKP, 1971).

A Dictionary of Symbols, J. E. Cirlot (RKP, 1962).

The Dragon and the Disc, F. W. Holiday (Sidgwick & Jackson, 1973).

English Romanesque Sculpture, 1066-1140, and *Later English Romanesque Sculpture*, George Zarnecki (Tiranti, 1951 and 1953).

The Evolution of the Dragon, G. Elliott Smith (Manchester University Press, Longmans, Green & Co., 1919).

Feng Shui, E. J. Eitel (republished Cockaygne, 1973).

Folklore of Hampshire and the Isle of Wight, Wendy Boase (Batsford, 1976).

Folklore of the Northern Counties, William Henderson (Longman, Green & Co., 1866), and revised edition (W. Satchell Peyton & Co., 1879).

Saint George of Lydda: Luzac's Semitic text in *Ethiopic Texts and Translations*, Sir E. A. Wallis Budge, 1930.

The Golden Bough, Sir James Frazer (Macmillan, 1922).

Greek Mythology, John Pinsent.

A Guide to Occult Britain, John Wilcock (Sidgwick & Jackson, 1976).

The Lost Gods of England, Brian Branston (Thames & Hudson, 1957).

Man and his Symbols, C. G. Jung.

Mazes and Labyrinths, W. H. Matthews (Longmans, 1922; Dover (USA), 1970).

Mysterious Britain, Janet and Colin Bord (Paladin, 1974).

The Mystic Spiral, Jill Purce (Thames & Hudson, 1975).

Myth and Ritual in Christianity, Alan Watts (Thames & Hudson, 1959).

Prelude to Chemistry - An Outline of Alchemy, John Read (M.I.T. Press, 1966).

The Paradise Papers, Merlin Stone (Virago Press, 1975).

The Secret Country, Janet and Colin Bord (Elek Books, 1976).

Thespis, Theodor Gaster (Schuman (New York), 1950).

Unnatural History, Colin Clair (Abelard-Schuman, 1968).

View Over Atlantis, John Michell (Sago, 1969).

Index

Gothic Image Publications

We are a Glastonbury based Imprint dedicated to publishing books and pamphlets which offer a new and radical approach to our perception of the world in which we live.

As ideas about the nature of life change, we aim to make available those new perspectives which clarify our understanding of ourselves and the Earth we share.

Glastonbury Tor Maze	£2.25
Glastonbury, Maker of Myths	£4.95
The Glastonbury Festivals	£6.95
Devas, Fairies and Angels	£3.50
Meditation in a Changing World	£6.95
Spiritual Dowsing	£5.50
Needles of Stone Revisited	£6.95
The Green Lady and The King of Shadows	£4.95
Hargreave's New Modern Bestiary	£9.95
Eclipse of the Sun	£8.95

These titles are available direct from Gothic Image, 7 High Street, Glastonbury, Somerset BA6 9DP, UK. Telephone: (0458) 31453.

Add 20% for postage and packing, 40% for Air Mail USA and Canada.

We also produce a mail order list of the best in alternative books . . . . . . and we organise tours of Ancient Sites in Britain and Ireland.

Write to us for further information.